Bobby Owsinski's

GW01045645

The Cruise Vacation FAQ Book

109 Questions and Answers About Booking, Boarding, Cruising and Dining On Your Next Cruise

The Cruise Vacation FAQ Book

109 Questions and Answers About Booking, Boarding, Cruising and Dining on Your Next Cruise
by Bobby Owsinski

Published by:
Bobby Owsinski Media Group
4109 West Burbank, Blvd.
Burbank, CA 91505

© Bobby Owsinski 2016
ISBN 13: 978-0-9888391-6-8

Please note that much of this publication is based on personal experience and anecdotal evidence. Although the author and publisher have made every reasonable attempt to achieve complete accuracy of the content in this Book, they assume no responsibility for errors or omissions. Also, you should use this information as you see fit, and at your own risk. Your particular situation may not be exactly suited to the examples illustrated herein; in fact, it's likely that they won't be the same, and you should adjust your use of the information and recommendations accordingly.

Any trademarks, service marks, product names or named features are assumed to be the property of their respective owners, and are used only for reference. There is no implied endorsement if we use one of these terms.

Finally, nothing in this Book is intended to replace common sense, legal, medical or other professional advice, and is meant to inform and entertain the reader.

To buy books in quantity for corporate use or incentives, call 818.588.6606 or email office@bobbyowsinski.com.

———————

Table Of Contents

Introduction

....

6

Booking Tips and Secrets   8

What Makes A Cabin Desirable?   32

Getting To The Ship On Time   44

Secrets To Boarding The Ship   54

Cruising Made Easy   58

The Ins and Outs of Cruise Ship Dining 74

To Love or Hate The Drink Package   80

Be Loyal To The Loyalty Program   84

What If Something Happens?   90

What About The Crew?   103

About Bobby Owsinski   114

Introduction

I love cruising. By the time you read this I'll be on at least cruise #19 across four different cruise lines on a wide variety of itineraries. I've learned a lot in that time, but the more I've cruised, the more questions I've had about it as well, just like you probably have if you've cruised before.

When you first begin to cruise, everything is a big question because you've not experienced it before, but as you do it more, your questions become more specific to your observations. How do I upgrade to a better cabin after I've paid for my cruise? Where does the crew live and much do they get paid? What happens if we sail into a hurricane? What's the hierarchy in the crew of the ship? Is a drink package worth it? These were just some of the questions that I had that really bugged me.

They bugged a lot of other people too, by the looks of the many online cruise forums, which are teaming with the same questions as you'll find in the book asked a multitude of different ways over and over again. You can get some answers on a forum, but you'll also get a lot of misinformation there as well.

As a result, I decided to find the answers to my many questions myself, and along the way incorporate as many of the typical cruise questions of both new and veteran cruisers as I could, with the hopes of providing some real go-to information if and when of the inevitable questions arises.

The Cruise Vacation FAQ book came about on my way to write a more complete guide to cruising, and my information comes from interviews with travel agents, cruise executives, ship captains, hotel managers and staff (you'll be able to read those entire interviews when that book is released), so you're getting the info from the horse's mouth, so to speak.

One thing that's different about this book from a lot of the other cruise books that I've read is that I try not to give an opinion, just the facts. I'll tell you the advantages and disadvantages of each situation or question, and you can decide what's best for you.

No two cruises, or cruisers for that matter, are ever alike, so the best thing you can have is the right data to make an informed decision on your own.

Another thing I'd caution is to not take the comments (especially the negative ones) on any of the forums on sites like Cruise Critic too seriously. Remember that things that some people absolutely hate are just the things that other people love. In fact, the opinions can be so different that I sometimes wonder if the cruisers that had such terrible negative experiences actual cruised on the same ship at the same time as the ones that proclaimed their cruise to be just great.

Finally, let me repeat the old adage that I'm sure you'll agree with - Even the worst cruise is better than a day at home! Enjoy your next cruise!

———

Chapter 1

Booking Tips and Secrets

Maybe the most difficult part of a cruise is actually booking it. For a cruise newbie there are a lot of unfamiliar terms and concepts to deal with, while cruise veterans want to know more about how to get the the best cabin for the best price. This chapters answers those questions.

#1: *When's the best time to book a cruise?*

Finding a cruise deal is almost a game for some people since the prices can change in the blink of an eye, sometimes with a low price posted in the morning that's gone in the afternoon, just like with the airlines. That said, most sales will last longer than that, some for a few days, and some for a few weeks.

There are usually two great times to book a cruise - somewhere around nine months to a year or more out, or right before sailing. Right before sailing means anywhere from 90 days (after the final payment has been made for people with reservations) to up to a few days before the ship sails. Reservations are closed the day before the ship sails in the United States as the passenger manifest must be prepared for the Coast Guard and US Immigration.

That said, deals can be had at any time period in between, usually depending upon how well the bookings for a cruise are going. And the sales don't always revolve around the posted price either. Sometimes the second passenger in the cabin will be half-off or even free, sometimes onboard credit will be included, sometimes it might mean a free drink package or spa session is included. Sometimes the price might be cheaper if you're a past customer, veteran, over 55 or even from a certain state. It's almost like booking a flight in that the price changes so frequently that you have make the decision to either keep up, or just book it and forget it like many cruisers do.

#2: *When are the busy and slow seasons?*

If you want to save some money, it's best to pick a time during the off-peak seasons. Here are the busiest and slowest times for a number of popular destinations to help you decide when you might want to look for cruise deals.

Destination	Busy Season	Slow Season
Caribbean	February to the end of July	August to December
Alaska	June to August	May and September
Australia	Mid-November to March	May to September
Bermuda	June to-August	April/May and September/October
Canada and New England	September and October	May to August
Northern Europe	June to August	May and September
Hawaii	January to April	May/June and September to December

Destination	Busy Season	Slow Season
Mediterranean	May to September	October to April
Tahiti	May to October	November to April

#3: *Can I get a deal on a holiday cruise?*

Some of the busiest and most expensive times to book a cruise are during just about any holiday throughout the year since more people have time off then. While it's not impossible to get a deal, the odds are against it because most holiday cruises are sold out well before they sail. The prices are almost always higher as well.

#4: *What's the most popular cruise destination?*

The itinerary of the cruise is a big deal for some and not so much for others. Many have been to the same ports of call multiple, even dozens of time (I've been to the Bahamas five times and Cozumel eight) but that just means that they find something new to do each time there, or stay on the ship while it's in port and enjoy the peace and quiet as most passengers enjoy the port.

That said, cruise itineraries for the major cruise lines are broken down into the following areas:

- Caribbean (the most popular), which can be further broken down even further to Southern, Western and Eastern.
- Mexico
- Alaska
- The Mediterranean
- Europe
- The Baltic
- Hawaii
- Bermuda
- Bahamas
- South Pacific
- South America
- Pacific Northwest
- Canada/New England
- Australia/New Zealand
- Repositioning

Most recently Dubai, the Middle East, China, and now Cuba have been added to the above, although most cruise lines are just gearing up for these new locations.

The Caribbean remains the leading cruise destination, garnering about 35% of all cruisers, followed by the

Mediterranean, Europe, Australia/New Zealand/Pacific, Alaska and South America.

> *TIP: While deals can be had for any itinerary, you'll see more in the Caribbean because of the sheer number of cruises that go there.*

#5: *What's better - a large or small ship?*

Cruise ships come in all sizes and in the case of the largest vessels like the Royal Caribbean's 6,296 passenger Oasis of The Seas, which can be a destination in itself where the itinerary matters little. These floating cities are amazing feats of engineering that have so much to do onboard that you may never want to get off at a port. It's not uncommon to hear a passenger comment about spending an entire week onboard and still not seeing everything that the ship had to offer.

Be aware that you pay a premium for a destination-type ship, as you do for a bright and shiny new one that's less than two years old. The older the vessel, the less expensive the fare becomes even though it may be fresh out of dry dock and completely refurbed.

That doesn't mean that you won't find tons of things to do on an older ship. These days, 10 years is considered older, although the ship life may be far beyond that before it, as they say, is "turned into nails." It just means that the ship most likely won't have the very latest and greatest features.

Most people find what's onboard beyond acceptable. It's like the difference between a brand new car with all the latest features, and clean low-miler from a couple of years ago. There are usually one or two features on the new one that the old one doesn't have (although those features might be spectacular), but it will still get you to where you want to go.

Another thing to consider when choosing a ship is that bigger is not always better, as smaller cruise ships are able to go to places where the larger ones cannot. That means that more exotic destinations are available, especially ports that don't have the docking facilities and draft that one of the behemoths requires. Also, some people just like the intimacy of a small cruise ship.

#6: *How much of a deposit do I have to put down to book a cruise?*

Most cruise lines ask for a small deposit of $100 to $250 if you book far enough ahead, although this depends upon the cruise line and itinerary. If you book within a certain window, they may ask for 50% down, and if you book within the last 90 days you'll be expected to pay the entire fare at once. *Keep in mind that the deposit for suites can be twice that or more than for lower cabin types.*

An advantage of booking ahead with a small deposit is that you don't tie up a lot of money while securing your fare rate and cabin. It also allows you to change cruise itineraries or even cancel altogether if you want. In many cases you'll get your deposit back, and in the cases where you don't, at least you won't be out that much.

> *TIP: Cruise lines usually want full payment 90 days from sailing, and will automatically pull the balance from the credit card that you paid your deposit with on that day, so be sure to make any changes to your reservation before then.*

#7: Do I get a better deal if I purchase a future cruise while onboard my current one?

In some cases, booking your next cruise while on board your current one is a good way to save money, and in other cases not so much. All ships have a number of cruise consultants available that you can meet with to discuss future cruises. They'll also provide a number of presentations during the course of a cruise to provide you with an overview of the cruise line's destinations or new ships in order to give you an idea of what's in store and perhaps entice you to make a reservation.

Be aware that you don't normally get a great price when booking onboard, but you do get some sort of extra onboard credit to use on that cruise, plus you give first choice of the available cabins. The onboard credit ranges anywhere from $25 to $500 or even more when booking a suite on a voyage 10 days or longer.

Many cruise lines don't even ask you to select a particular voyage, and only want you to provide a deposit of $100 that promises that you will be sailing with them in the next 18 months. That's a pretty good deal in that you can then choose a booking at a later time when there's a good deal to be had.

I used to use this booking method quite a bit until Royal Caribbean changed its policy to where you had to select the cruise that you wanted in order to get a reasonable amount of credit. Of course you can always change the cruise later, but to many it hardly seems worth the effort considering that the credit is lower than it use to be. Plus, you'll being spending time either waiting until the cruise consultant finishes with another client or just going through the paperwork of booking, which takes time away from the cruise that you're on. The credit better be worth the effort for that.

#8: *Can I make changes to my reservation after I paid for it in full?*

Yes, but it will cost you if you're changing dates or itineraries. Your previous reservation may have to be cancelled and a new one will cause you to be charged at the going rate of the day, which may be more than you previously paid. Plus, you may lose any onboard credit as well.

Changing cabins is different. If you find a better deal on your currently booked cruise that what you paid, you can request an upgrade to the better cabin class. You won't be charged if you paid more than the current price, or you may have to pay a small difference if the price is higher.

#9: *Can I get a refund if my room goes for a cheaper price after I paid for it in full?*

Let's say that you've made the final payment on your cruise yesterday, but spot a huge discount on the exact same cabin category on today's cruise line newsletter. You're angry because you've paid hundreds of dollars more than the sale price so you get on the phone with the cruise line to demand the difference back.

Save your breath, no cruise line will give you a full refund after you've made the final payment. What they will do is allow you to upgrade to a higher class cabin, say one with a balcony or a suite. If the upgraded cabin price is less than what you've already paid, you get the better cabin if it's available for no charge. Sometimes the price difference for the better cabin is just a little higher that what you've already paid and is worth the small extra fee to upgrade.

For example, let's say you originally booked an inside cabin at $789 per person. After final payment you see the same class cabin is now available for $599, but an outside cabin is now available for $769 and a balcony cabin is $819. You won't be able to get a credit for the difference between the new price and what you paid, but you could upgrade to the outside cabin and not pay any more out of pocket (although it's now $20 per person less than what you originally paid), or you can spend the extra $30 per person for a far better balcony cabin.

The trick is that you won't get this upgrade automatically so be prepared to call either your travel agent if that's where you booked the cruise, or your cruise line if you booked it directly, and ask for the upgrade. If available, it's a simple change.

Keep in mind that there's probably a good possibility that the price will change on your cruise after the 90 day mark, which is why some people wait until closer to embarkation to make their purchase. That said, a price drop is not automatic. In fact, it may never drop at all, so you could be stuck with a cabin that you might not like if you wait too long to book.

#10: *What is onboard credit?*

Many cruise lines and travel agents will offer something called onboard credit as a booking bonus, which is a credit against any charges that you make while on the ship. This means that if you have a $100 onboard credit, the first $100 you spend during your cruise is automatically paid regardless of what you purchase. It may be applied to anything from drinks to the spa to specialty dining to the daily crew tips that accrue to your account. You can't specify exactly what to spend it on, it just comes off the top of your bill.

The only thing that onboard credit doesn't apply to is anything that is prepaid before you embark, such as prepaid gratuities, excursions or specialty dining reservations that are booked ahead of when you board the ship.

Onboard credit comes in increments as small as $25 and can go as high as $500 or even more. You may get it by purchasing the cruise by a given date, purchasing your next cruise while onboard your current cruise, or as an enticement for selecting a higher class of cabin. It can come for each passenger or for each cabin, depending on the offer. However you get it, it means that you're getting a least a small discount on your cruise in the form of charges accrued onboard that you don't have to pay for.

#11: *What if I have excess onboard credit at the end of my cruise?*

Depending upon the cruise line, you might get the difference back in cash, you might be able to apply it to your next cruise, or you might lose the difference completely. It doesn't happen often, but if you think you'll have an excess at the end of your cruise, check with guest relations to make sure you're not disappointed.

> *TIP: If you want to cash out your credit, many cruise lines will allow you to do so at the purser's office or in the casino. Keep in mind that the casino may charge a transaction fee of up to 5%.*

#12: *If I cruise by myself how much do I pay?*

Solo cruisers are penalized for going it alone since cruise lines have a minimum double occupancy for most cabins. If you cruise by yourself (as I usually do) you still pay for two. Sometimes there's a deal called a *single supplement* where you'll only be charged 175% or 150% of the full price instead of 200%, but you'll still be staying in a cabin designed for two.

Since more and more people are traveling solo these days, many of the newest ships are designed to have more cabins that can accommodate the solo traveler. These are sometimes called "studio" cabins, and many even open into a dedicated single's lounge.

This all sounds great for the solo traveler but the fact of the matter is that solo cabins are actually a problem for the cruise lines in that they take up almost as much space as a regular inside cabin with only a single revenue source instead of two. Since much of the revenue for both the ship and the hospitality crew comes from passengers, it's better for them to have two people in a room even at a deep discount rather than one at full price. As a result, don't expect to see a ship full of solo cabins anytime soon. Still, even having a few singles-oriented cabins is a step in the right direction for solo cruising.

#13: *What is the "upgrade fairy?"*

Cruise lines have been known to mysteriously upgrade people to a better cabin without them asking or sometimes even knowing. For cruise veterans, this is called a visit from the "upgrade fairy" and is one of the mysteries of cruising.

No one, and I mean absolutely no one outside of the cruise line operator, has a clue about how someone is chosen for an upgrade since the selection is so random. It could happen to an elite loyalty club member or a first time cruiser, you just never know. It could happen weeks before the cruise or you can find out that your cabin has been changed when you check in at the dock. Some people go their entire cruising career over dozens of cruises and never have it happen while others get lucky right at the beginning.

If you do get a visit from the upgrade fairy, cherish the moment because it doesn't happen very often.

#14: *Can I cruise with an infant?*

Yes, but most cruise lines want baby to be at least 6 months so make sure that your baby is 6 months old and not a few days short of that. On some cruise lines, junior must be 12 months old to sail on any itinerary with more than 2 sea days in a row or anything longer than 7 days

Another thing to remember is that babies cost as much as an adult as the third person in the room, although sometimes there are sales where kids sail free. Also, Junior won't be allowed near the pool unless he is fully potty trained.

The good thing is that many ships have a nursery onboard and even in-room babysitting as well as programs for babies up to 3 years old, so you'll be able to get a break for a bit.

Here are some helpful hits and tips for cruise with a baby:

1. Take anything you might need for the child with you. You won't find much that will work in the ship's store, and even if they do have something you need in stock, the stores aren't open 24/7 or while in port, and the costs can be prohibitive.

2. If you are flying to your embarkation city, pad in a day or two to do some shopping for items you didn't want to pack, like extra diapers, formula, etc.

3. Remember that there's very little extra room in most cabins for a full-size stroller.

#15: *Can I add or subtract names from a reservation?*

Often times there's a lot of uncertainty whether the additional people on a reservation will actually make it. That can force you into a conundrum, especially if you see a great deal on a cruise that you know won't last very long. The question then becomes, do I reserve for everyone now or wait until later to add the people to my reservation once they confirm they're actually going?

It's usually better to book the other people or additional cabins now, either under your name or with a TBA (to be announced). This is fairly common, especially in the case of a couple who are expecting a baby and book a cruise a year out. They have no idea what the name or the actual birthdate is going to be.

To add someone to the reservation at a later time is certainly doable, but that person will not get the advantage of the price that you paid, and must pay whatever the rate is on the day they're added, which could be substantially higher.

It's always easier to delete a person or cabin from the booking than to add one. That said, some cruise lines might reprice the entire booking as a result, so be sure to ask what might happen before you make your initial reservation.

Sometimes you want to book a group of people who are connected together like a church group, office or sports team where one person makes the reservation, but each passenger or couple pays for their own cabin. Once again, you may not have to have all the names in place when the initial booking is placed.

#16: Is there a discount if I book a block of rooms?

One of the advantages of booking a group is that you get a discount for each block of cabins that are booked. This could mean either a free cabin reservation or the cash equivalent. The person booking the group can either keep it for herself as a reward for the hassle involved or spread it out evenly among the group.

Most cruise lines also realize that the needs and means of the people in the group are different, so you can mix and match the cabin types as needed, meaning inside, outside, balcony or suite.

Just like with smaller reservations that are tied together, group reservations are also tied together so that restaurant and excursions are together as well. As a perk, groups may even be given the use of one of the ship's onboard conference rooms in the Conference Center as well if that's needed during the cruise.

You can book a group with your travel agent or you can go to the special group consultant that the cruise line provides that will help with each group booking.

#17: Do I have to use a travel agent?

There are two schools of thought as to whether to book a cruise through a travel agent or directly through the cruise line. Some people feel more comfortable with their local travel agent or specialty agent online who may be able to intercede on their behalf with the various travel companies, while others feel they'd rather not have a middleman in between them and the cruise line.

One of the things in favor of travel agents is that they sometimes have better deals than the advertised rates of the cruise lines because the agency bought a block of rooms, and may also add extra onboard credit or even a bottle of wine to the mix too. While this sounds good, there's always a caveat involved in that sometimes onboard credits are not combinable, so the $100 you receive from the cruise line won't be added to the $125 from the travel agent, or vice versa. Then again, sometimes they are and you have a nice extra sum of money to play with on board. It just depends upon the cruise.

Many cruisers like to book via the online specialty cruise agents like Vacations To Go, CruCon or CruisesOnly. They all operate a little differently, in that some make it easier to dial up an itinerary online, while others show more precisely which rooms are available. In some cases you never have to even speak with a person to book the cruise, although it's advisable that you do since you may be able to get an extra discount that you didn't know existed, especially if you're a returning customer.

You can actually use a combination of both direct and travel agent as well, first starting the booking yourself and then transferring it to a travel agent later. This is an option when booking your next cruise while you're on board your current one where you're dealing directly with the cruise line.

> *TIP: While you can transfer a booking to a travel agent, you can't go the other way and transfer from a travel agent back to the cruise line.*

#18: *Do I have to book port excursions through the ship?*

No, you can book excursions independently and many cruisers choose to do so. Sometimes the independent excursions are more interesting and usually they're cheaper than through the ship. Most of the indie excursion operators have been doing it a long time and have numerous reviews online to check out.

One of the downsides of using an indie operator is that since he's not tied to the ship, you risk getting left behind if you're late for any reason, something that won't happen with a ship-sponsored excursion. That said, most legit operators have good tics with the cruise line and are very aware of the time, and will call the ship to give them an ETA if they happen to run late.

#19: *Is cruise insurance worth it?*

Some feel it's worth it and others don't. The trick is the kind of insurance that you buy. Some policies are limited in their coverage while others are more comprehensive "cancel for any reason" policies that are more expensive. Usually you have to purchase these policies within 15 days of booking your cruise.

If you're ill and unsure how you'll feel when cruise time comes around, some insurance policies cover pre-existing conditions while others don't, so you have to be very specific with what you want, then weigh the costs versus the benefits. If a policy costs as much as your cruise, then it's obviously not a great deal.

> *TIP: Trip insurance is offered through the cruise line, but you can usually get a better deal elsewhere at about half the cost if you shop a little. Some sites to check out that have gotten good reviews include insuremytrip.com, squaremouth.com, quotewrite.com and TripInsuranceStore.com.*

#20: *Is there a service that monitors cruise prices?*

It can be exhausting checking cruise prices every day, but there are a few ways to be automatically alerted when a fare does drop. One way is to use the free tool on CruiseCritic.com, which compares cruise prices with the highest published rates over the previous seven days.

Another popular method is a service called Cruisefish, which provides unlimited monitoring of all cabin categories for a single sail date. Each date costs $0.99 USD or less if you buy them in bulk. It's a small investment that can save you hundreds of dollars on your cruise.

Crusiefaremonitor has another site where you pay one fee and get unlimited daily monitoring and unlimited alerts if the cost of your stateroom (per person) drops below the price you originally paid.

#21: *Can I book an early flight home when the cruise is over?*

Most cruises officially arrive back in their home ports at 7 or 8AM. While it might seem feasible to book a 10AM flight home, there are a number of things to consider that might impact when you actually arrive at the airport.

First, if you have a lot of luggage and can't carry it off the ship yourself, you're forced to wait your turn to disembark. The ship splits the passengers into groups depending upon your cabin type, loyalty tier and location. You're then asked to join your group in an area of the ship where you'll wait until it's your time to leave. You might get lucky and get an early group that gets you off in an hour, but you could also get a group that isn't scheduled to leave until 10AM so you'll miss your flight. You can ask the front desk for an early departure so you can catch your plane, but there are other factors involved that you have to account for.

For one thing, your place in the early disembark line can make a difference. Even if you choose to carry your bags off for an early disembark, people begin lining up even before the ship docks, so chances are there'll be a hundred or more people ahead of you. This line could go surprisingly fast, or it can snake along at a snails pace.

The next hurdle is Customs and Immigration, where you're guaranteed to face another more formidable line. If there are only two agents on duty to pass 3,000 passengers, you might be waiting for an hour or more. This is why they stagger the disembark by scheduling groups at 15 minute intervals.

One thing that no one can prepare for is the Coast Guard holding up the disembark until it clears the ship. If there's something out of line with the manifest, the condition of the ship, or a suspected sickness outbreak, the Guard can hold everything up until it's satisfied that it's safe to disembark. I had this happen to me once where we were held up for two hours before the first passengers could leave.

Finally there's the trip to the airport. No matter how close the airport is to the port, remember that you're going to be traveling during morning rush hour if you leave first thing after the ship docks. That could add a lot of time to the trip even with an aggressive cab driver.

That's why it's best to schedule your flight back home for noon or later. Give yourself some time in case the schedule doesn't work out as planned.

———————

Chapter 2

What Makes A Cabin Desirable?

On your first cruise you're only aware of the four basic types of cabins; inside, outside, balcony and suite. After you've cruised for a while however, you realize that there are real differences within those categories. The problem is that the information on those differences may not be readily available, and each cruise line has a different way to classify them anyway. This chapter is all about discovering which is the most desirable cabins of each category, and which one is right for you.

#22: *What's the difference between cabin classes?*

Within the types of cabins there are subcategories called *classes* that generally reflect the desirability of a cabin. These classes can be difficult to navigate sometime, like being given a choice between a class H and a class B cabin and having no idea what that means. Let's see if we can bring some clarity to the situation.

Different cruise lines categorize their cabins differently. Let's look at the two largest, Carnival and Royal Caribbean, as a comparison.

Carnival

On Carnival the lower the letter, in the alphabet, the more desirable the cabin is. For instance, a 4H is more desirable than a 4B. Here's a list of cabin classes and their attributes.

Class	Style	Area	Description
1A	Inside Cabin	185 sq.ft	Odd shaped, but least expensive. Can accommodate 2.
4A through H	Inside Cabin	185 sq.ft	Some can accommodate up to 4
4J	Outside Cabin	185 sq.ft	Obstructed view

Class	Style	Area	Description
6A through 6C	Outside Cabin	185 sq.ft	Some can accommodate up to 4
7A	Balcony Cabin	185 sq.ft with 40 sq. ft. balcony	Obstructed view. Some can accommodate up to 4
8A through 8F	Balcony Cabin	185 sq.ft with 40 sq. ft. balcony	Some can accommodate up to 4
8k	Balcony Cabin	185 sq.ft with 60 to 180 sq. ft. balcony	Extended balcony
8M and 8N	Balcony Cabin	185 sq.ft with 60 sq. ft. balcony	Aft view. Some can accommodate up to 4
9A	Balcony Cabin	230 sq.ft with 55 sq. ft. balcony	Premium. Obstructed view.
9B and 9C	Balcony Cabin	230 sq.ft with 85 sq. ft. balcony	Premium
JS	Junior Suite	275 sq. ft/ 40 sq. ft balcony	Walk-in closet, whirlpool tub, living room with desk. Can accommodate 2.

Class	Style	Area	Description
OS	Ocean View Suite	275 sq. ft with 220 sq. ft balcony	Walk-in closet, whirlpool tub, living room with desk. Some can accommodate up to 4.
VS	Vista Suite	45 sq. ft/ 220 sq. fit balcony	Walk-in closet, whirlpool tub, living room with desk. Some can accommodate up to 3.
GS	Grand Suite	300 sq. ft/ 115 sq. ft balcony	Walk-in closet, whirlpool tub, living room with desk. Some can accommodate up to 4.

Royal Caribbean

Royal has a lot more designations and we won't get into them all, plus they've just recategorized them effective April 2015. Unlike Carnival, the lower the number or letter, the more desirable a room. For instance, a K category room is more desirable than an M, and a D1 is better than a D3.

Class	Style	Area	Description
M, N and Q	Inside	160	Double occupancy

Class	Style	Area	Description
L	Inside	160	Some can accommodate up to 4
PR	Inside	167	Promenade view.
FO	Ocean View	265	Large window
E1, E2	Balcony	220	Deluxe. Some can accommodate up to 4.
E3	Balcony	220	Deluxe. Double occupancy
D1	Balcony	238	Superior. Some can accommodate up to 4
D2, D3	Balcony	238	Superior. Can accommodate 2.
G	Ocean View	180	Obstructed view
F, H, K	Ocean View	180	Some can accommodate up to 4
JS	Junior Suite	376	Balcony sitting area with sofa, 2 twin beds or 1 queen-size bed, refrigerator or minibar, private bathroom with bathtub
GS	Grand Suite	476	sitting area with sofa, 2 twin beds or 1 queen-size bed, concierge service, minibar, private bathroom with bathtub

Class	Style	Area	Description
FS	Family Suite	610	Living area with double sofa bed, 2 bedrooms with 2 twin beds or 1 queen-size bed (one room with third and fourth Pullman beds), concierge service, minibar, concierge service, 2 bathrooms (one with a shower the other with a bathtub)
OS	Owners Suite	570	Separate living area with queen size sofa bed, additional queen -size bed, minibar, concierge service, walk-in closet, private bathroom with whirlpool tub and shower
RS	Royal Suite	1066	Balcony with hot tub, separate bedroom with king-size bed, living room with queen-size sofa bed, baby grand piano, wet bar, dining table, concierge service, private bathroom with whirlpool tub and shower

NOTE: These charts are must meant to give you a general idea of the classes and how they work. Cruise lines change their classes all the time, so these may no longer be relevant by the time you read this. They also add and subtract and predesignate classes as well.

> TIP: *It sometimes helps to bring something like a ribbon for the doorknob or a postcard that can be clipped to the paper slot to act as a landmark to help you find your room.*

#23: *What's the best part of the ship to be in if you get seasick?*

If you tend to get seasick, you probably want a cabin towards the middle of the ship and on a lower deck. That way you're near the center of the ship's gravity and will experience the least amount of roll if the seas get a little rough.

#24: *What's the best deck to be on?*

To some cruisers the deck selection is a matter of convenience and for others it's a matter of prestige, but most people would rather be up on the higher decks than the lower ones. While the lower decks might be better for those who are prone to motion sickness, for the most part they also mean a longer trip to the top pool and entertainment decks, although clubs and restaurants are located on different decks throughout the ship.

Lower decks are usually less expensive and can be a lot quieter since the noise from the venues, casinos and restaurants, not to mention the joggers and people moving pool chairs, are located far away.

Many cruisers looking for the most peace and quiet will try to select a cabin on a deck where there are also cabins directly above and below, which also usually means a lower deck.

#25: *What's a guaranteed cabin?*

A *guaranteed cabin* selection is one where you make a reservation for the class of cabin that you want, but you let the cruise line pick the exact cabin location for you. Many times you won't even know your room number or your deck until you check-in.

For a lower price, the cruise line guarantees that you'll get at least the cabin category that you selected, and you might luck out and even get an upgrade to a better room. The guarantee is that you'll never get a lower category than what you paid for.

Now if you're thinking that if you select a guaranteed inside cabin and might end up with a suite instead, just stop right there since this scenario rarely happens. What might happen is that you might get a better location, a larger cabin, or you might even be upgraded to the next class of cabin, but you probably won't be upgraded beyond the next category level.

The other problem with booking a guaranteed cabin is that the location of the cabin can be a big deal to some cruisers, as you've just read. By selecting the guaranteed category, your cabin location is a roll of the dice, and you won't be able to change it either. For the extra couple of bucks that it saves, you're better off just selecting the cabin that best suits your needs when you book your cruise.

#26: *What's an obstructed view cabin?*

Many cabins are what's known as *obstructed view* which means that the view either out the porthole or balcony is limited for some reason. This might be because there's some part of the ship's infrastructure or lifeboat in the way, or it may face out the promenade deck (keep those shades drawn) where people are constantly walking by. There will usually be a deal on these kinds of rooms if you're willing to live with the limited view.

> *TIP: Sometimes obstructed view cabins are sold as inside cabins. These are called secret porthole cabins by veteran cruisers and can usually be identified on the various ships by visiting one of the many online cruise forums (especially CruiseCritic.com).*

#27: *What's a virtual balcony?*

A new feature on some premium Royal Caribbean inside cabins is what they call a virtual balcony. This is a floor to ceiling television monitor permanently connected to a camera outside the ship. There's also a speaker so that you hear the sounds happening outside the ship where the camera is pointed at. You have the option to turn the screen or the audio off if you find it distracting.

While a virtual balcony can be kind of cool during the day, it's virtually useless at night as all you see is black, although you can hear the sound of the ship driving through the ocean. I personally like this feature a lot, but wouldn't pay much extra for it, since it really doesn't add all that much to the experience of the cruise in my opinion.

> *TIP: Inside cabins can be found on any deck of the ship, with the ones on upper decks slightly more desirable and therefore slightly more expensive.*

#28: *Are balcony cabins windy?*

Forward balcony rooms (the first quarter of the ship or so) will have a lot more wind than those further back. Some balconies near the very front will be very cool and extremely windy most of the time when the ship is at sea. That said, all side balconies will get some sort of a breeze, even the ones near the back of the ship, except for aft balconies which tend to have no wind at all and, as a result, can get hot quickly.

#29: *What's the difference between the different types of suites that are available?*

Modern cruise ships feature a variety of suites that go from just a step above a standard balcony cabin to almost a condo at sea at two stories, multiple bedrooms, more than 2,000 square feet of space, and even a private attendant.

One of the reasons that suites are so popular is that not only do they feature more room and lush furnishings, but also include a variety of extra services and amenities. These range from concierge service, priority embarkation and disembarkation, and assistance when making reservations for the ship's specialty restaurants, spa, shore excursions and even airline travel. Butler service is offered with the ultra high-end suites, and they'll handle everything from dry-cleaning and unpacking to daily delivery of hors d'oeuvres and fresh fruit and flowers.

Another perk of booking a suite is that you'll get extra points awarded in the cruise line's royalty program. These points vary with each cruise line, but may amount to double what you'd normally be awarded in a lower class cabin.

Suites range from the junior or mini-suite to full-on family suites that can accommodate up to eight people. Of course the price of a suite is commensurate with the luxury it offers and can go anywhere from $500 per person per night up to $1,500 or more.

TIP: Usually suites are the first to go on sale along with inside cabins, and suite discounts are among the most popular bargains that are scooped up immediately by cruisers if the price is right.

#30: *What is a junior suite?*

A junior suite is a mini-suite that may be nothing more than an extended balcony cabin with maybe 50% more space. What's more, it might not even come with many of the amenities of the other suites on the ship. You'll still be awarded extra points in the loyalty program however.

#31: *What does "on the hump" mean?*

Many veteran cruises aim for cabins with balconies "on the hump," which is the area at the center of the ship where it bulges out from the rest of the ship. The reason is that you tend to get a better view both fore and aft than on balconies located elsewhere on the ship.

———

Chapter 3

Getting To The Ship On Time

You've booked your dream cruise, now it's time to board the ship. Most of the time it's easy, but there are still ways to make sure you maximize your vacation by gaining every minute available onboard. Here are the most common questions and situations that pop up when you get to check-in at the port.

#32: *What time should I be at the port for my cruise?*

Most cruises leave between 4PM and 5PM, although some may not leave port until midnight depending upon the itinerary or local weather conditions. That said, you want to get started on your vacation as soon as you can so it's best to get a head start by getting there early.

Most cruises will begin to let new passengers on board around 11AM providing that all the passengers from the previous cruise have disembarked. Your stateroom may not be ready yet so some cruise lines won't let you in your room until around 1PM, but you can still get lunch, a drink, or just sit by the pool and relax. You've paid for it, so you might as well get started as soon as you can.

There are occasions where the cruise line will text or email you with a later time to embark. Usually this has to do with weather or a repair, but I once got an email asking me to check in at 7PM instead of earlier because the ship was being sanitized because of a norovirus outbreak (the ship was departed at 10PM instead of the normal 4PM). When I arrived there was a massive line to get on the ship - longer than anything I've ever encountered. I was later told that the people that ignored the email and showed up earlier in the day just walked right on with no delay. The morale is to take those "arrive later" emails with a grain of salt.

> *TIP: No matter how many times you've cruised before, it's a good idea to have the boarding pictures taken by the photographer on the gangway, even if you have absolutely no intention of buying them. Many of the newer ships have facial recognition systems that will include any other pictures you take for the remainder of the cruise in the same "folder." Even if your cruise card isn't properly registered when a subsequent photo is taken by any of the ship's many photographers, the photo won't get lost if that first one is tied to your account.*

#33: *What's the latest time I can get to the port?*

You must check in at least one hour before the ship departs. This is because a passenger manifest must go to the Coast Guard and U.S. Immigration prior to the ship leaving. If you get there 15 minutes before the ship sails, you're not getting on your cruise even though the ship hasn't left yet.

#34: *When's the best time to fly in for my cruise?*

If you're not within easy driving distance from the port that your ship is sailing from, you're going to have to fly into the nearest airport. Although most cruise lines also offer a full package that includes airfare, generally speaking it's been found to be financially beneficial only for international flights, and there's also the convenience factor of dealing directly with the airline rather than through a third party.

The advantage in using the cruise line's air reservation system is that the ship will know if you're flight is delayed and may delay departure until your arrival. If you can't make it in time, the cruise line will then make arrangements to get you to the next port of call so you can join the ship mid-cruise.

Regardless how you book your flight, the idea is to get to the port with enough time to check in. Here are some guidelines to get you to the port with plenty of time to spare so you can start enjoying your cruise as soon as possible.

- **Try to fly in the day before.** Sometimes this is the only option due to the flights available, but by flying in the day before you'll ensure that you'll get there on time even if there's an aircraft delay or cancellation.

- **Don't fly the same day as your cruise during the winter.** Even though you may be flying to and from a warm weather city, a winter storm somewhere else in the country or world can still play havoc with your flight plans.

- **Take a direct flight if at all possible.** Every connection you make increases the risk that you'll be delayed or your baggage won't arrive with you.

- **Take the first flight in the morning.** If you do fly the same day, the first flight of the day is usually on time since the aircraft is more likely to have spent the night at the airport.

Personally I'm a fan of the red eye flight when going coast to coast. It usually leaves anywhere from 10PM to 1AM from LAX and arrives in one of the Florida port cities at anywhere from 6AM to 11AM, depending upon if there are connections or not.

Remember to also take the transportation time from the airport to the port into account after your flight has arrived. Sometimes the airport is within a few minutes of the port like Fort Lauderdale or Miami, but other times it's an hour or so away like Hobby or George Bush International is to Galveston or Orlando International is to Port Canaveral. Make sure you leave some margin for error in your flight plans.

> *TIP: Many hotels close to the port will offer a cruise package to park your car for the duration of the cruise (if that's how you'll be traveling) and and some may even include an overnight stay. Most of these packages also include a shuttle to the ship.*

#35: Is there transportation from the airport to the port?

Virtually all cruise lines have multiple shuttles (buses) that will take you to and from the airport to the ship, usually for less than the cost of a cab. You may have to wait a while until the bus fills up, but you'll be sure to get to check-in at the cruise terminal in plenty of time.

You can usually book this shuttle reservation online with your cruise, but it's also possible to do a walk-on at the airport as well. Finding where it meets is pretty easy, as there are people with signs for the cruise line that will walk around baggage claim to guide you, and there will be a portable stand with the cruise line's name that's a meeting point where you can make the shuttle reservation. Keep in mind that these usually don't open until 9AM, so if your flight arrives at 5:45AM, prepare to get a nice long breakfast.

> *TIP: Most cruise lines won't allow you to book port transportation until you provide your airline reservation flight times. If you don't have your flights booked yet, supply a fake one (look up a flight that you're likely to take first) so you can book the shuttle, and just remember to change it later.*

#36: Can I cruise without a passport?

It depends. If you're a U.S. citizen and you board a cruise ship in a U.S. port that will travel only in the Western

Hemisphere and return to the same U.S. port, then yes, you can cruise without a passport if you have a copy of your birth certificate (or a Consular report of Birth Abroad, or Certificate of Naturalization) and another form of picture ID. This is what's known as a "closed-loop" cruise.

U.S. Citizen children under age 16 that arrive by sea from Canada, Mexico, Bermuda, or the Caribbean can present an original or certified copy of their birth certificate.

There are exceptions though, as Barbados, Guadeloupe, Haiti, Martinique, St. Barts, St. Martin, Trinidad and Tobago all require cruise passengers to have a valid passport in order to enter their countries. You can still sail on the cruise to these islands as long as you stay on the ship at these ports if you don't have a passport.

Remember, just because you can cruise without a passport doesn't mean that you should. If you miss the ship, trying to reenter the U.S. without one could be a nightmare that you don't want.

NOTE: Some countries require visas for entry. The cruise line can help you get the proper paperwork ahead of time, but it's essential to have these documents in place before you embark.

TIP: Many countries require that your passport be valid for at least six months beyond your cruise date before they allow entry.

#37: My passport is about to run out and I need a new one fast. What can I do?

You actually have a number of alternatives. The best bet is to make an appointment at one of the 28 U.S. passport agencies around the country. If you're not close to one, you can also do it by mail. The expedite cost is an additional fee of $60 on top of the passport fee of $110. You can also get overnight delivery for another additional charge.

You can also use one of the private services like rushmypassport.com or 24hourpassportsandvisas.com, but they'll charge an additional fee.

#38: Can I still get onboard if I forgot my passport?

Picture this harrowing scenario. You get to the cruise check-in counter excited that you're about to board this big beautiful ship on your long awaited vacation only to discover that you forgot your passport at home. Everyone from the cruise line is sympathetic, but they can't allow you to board without some sort of acceptable government issued identification because of U.S. Immigration law and Homeland Security rules.

You have two choices at this point. If you're at the embarkation city a day early (which many people will do), the easiest thing is to call a relative or friend and have them Fedex your passport overnight to you. If you need your passport on the same day, the only chance is to have your person at home deliver it to an Airline service like Delta Dash, who'll put it on the next direct flight to the city that you're in. Of course, this assumes that you live near a city with a major airport to begin with.

If you're boarding a ship in a US port and traveling to the Caribbean, Bahamas or Canada, you have another option. Get that relative or friend to make a copy of your birth certificate (or if born outside of the US, a Consular Report of Birth Abroad or Certificate of Naturalization) and fax it to the cruise line, who will be very helpful in expediting this on their end. You'll also need a government-issued photo ID like a driver's license, but this photocopy will now allow you to board.

Can't find your birth certificate? There's still a way out. You can call the city hall in your town or the Bureau of Vital Statistics for the state where you were born and ask them to make a duplicate of your birth certificate and either send or fax it to you. The problem is that the turnaround time (and cost) varies from state to state, so getting this done might not be as timely as you need.

There are online companies that can also obtain your birth certificate for you (USBirthCertificate.net and VitalChek.com are two of the bigger ones), but once again, they may also encounter the same bureaucratic delay, although they may also have ways to expedite it as well. It's also worth noting that some states like California are making it a lot more difficult to do this in an effort to thwart identify theft, and may require a notarized form before they begin the process.

One thing's for sure, if you don't have one of these documents, you won't be cruising. To make matters worse, the cruise line will only refund the port charges and not a penny of the cruise fare you paid, although some might offer to rebook you on a cruise at a latter time, probably with a penalty (don't count on this though).

———————

Chapter 4

Secrets To Boarding The Ship

Boarding the ship can be easy, but there's always a number of common questions that arise. Hopefully this chapter will answer them nicely.

#39: *How many bags can I bring on board?*

Unlike an airline there are no restrictions on the number of bags you can bring on board. Practically speaking though, there's only so much room in your cabin for both clothes and empty bags so you'll find that more than a couple will end up being an inconvenience. It's said that cruise lines begin to frown when the weight approaches 200 pounds.

Most veteran cruisers learn to pack lightly and can fit everything they need for a week in just one bag. It pays to heed the old cruise saying, "Bring half the clothes you think you'll need and twice the money."

#40: Can I bring alcohol onboard?

Most cruise lines will not allow any beer or hard liquor to be brought on board and will confiscate it at the security area. Most allow you to bring two bottles of wine per cabin onboard, although if you're cruising solo that number may be reduced to one.

Many people try to get around this by putting their booze in a water bottle or a Rum Runner (a plastic flask), but cruise ship security teams everywhere are hip to this and are pretty good at discovering them. You can try it, but it will probably just be a waste of good alcohol and get you a trip to the "naughty room." You won't get kicked off the cruise though.

#41: Can I bring soda or water onboard?

You're not supposed to be able to bring soda or water onboard but many security teams looks the other way. If you try to hide it in your luggage, it will most likely be flagged. If you're pretty blatant about it and just put a luggage tag on the case, it may get through without a mention. That said, sometimes security is really tight and they have no qualms about seizing it.

#42: *What is a muster drill and why do I have to do it?*

The muster drill is another name for a lifeboat drill, which in the U.S. occurs about a half-hour before the ship departs. That means that you must go to the staging area that you'll use if you ever have to abandon ship. Everyone hates it (especially the crew), but it's for your own good as you want to be familiar with the surroundings and procedures if a catastrophe should strike.

If you remember the Costa Concordia disaster of 2012, much of the chaos was caused by the fact that the muster drill didn't occur (it was to happen the following day after more passengers boarded) so people were totally unaware of where they should go or what they should do when the crisis erupted.

The muster drill may or may not include life jackets, depending upon the cruise line or ship. Some ships ask you to take the life jacket from your cabin, then show you how to put it on during the drill. Other cruise lines just want you to show up at your appointed muster station (the numbered location will be printed on your cruise card/cabin key and cabin door).

The muster drill is mandated by the Coast Guard and must occur before the ship can leave port in the U.S. In other parts of the world it must occur within the first 24 hours of sailing. Your attendance is mandatory, and the crew does a thorough room check to make sure that you don't try to skip out of it. It only takes about 15 minutes and then your cruise can really begin.

#43: *Can I skip the muster drill?*

No, it's mandatory and every passenger in every cabin must be accounted for before the captain releases pronounces the drill complete. If for some reason you do miss it, there is a make up drill that will occur later in the evening. Failure to attend both can mean being put off at the next port.

#44: *When can I get into my room when I board?*

It depends on the ship and when it arrived in port that morning. If the arrival was late or the guests were delayed in disembarking, chances are your room won't be immediately ready if you board early, so you'll have to wait while it's being prepared. This gives you time to have lunch and explore the ship. Most ships try to have the rooms available by at least 1PM.

Chapter 5

Cruising Made Easy

Finally your cruise has begun, but what about the kids, the drinks, the excursions and the way to pay for it all. Here are the answers to the most common cruise and excursion questions.

#45: Will I get bored while cruising?

Maybe if you stay in your room for the entire time and watch television, but there are so many things going on all day long that's its difficult to not find some activity that doesn't pique your interest. Plus, you go to an exciting new location almost every day that has new things to see and do. If you just want to relax, there's something so tranquil about watching the ocean that its fun just by itself. And you can't beat lying in the sun by the pool or just people watching in the dozens of public places of the ship.

#46: *Will my kids have enough to do onboard?*

Most likely yes, but how much depends upon the cruise line. Of course Disney is family oriented so keeping the kids amused is never a problem, but other lines like Carnival and Royal Caribbean have gone to great lengths to make their ships kid friendly too.

That means special dedicated areas for a particular age group. For instance, Royal Caribbean has the H2O zone, a dedicated aqua park for kids, as well as dedicated hangouts for teens, a video arcade, a teen spa, and dance and sport competitions. It also has areas for kids from 3 to 11 and a Babies and Tots program for those 6 months to 3 years old. Add to that waterpark adventures like Flowrider surfing and water slides, as well as rock climbing, basketball and mini-golf. There can be so much to do that some kids won't want to leave the ship.

#47: *Can I get away from the kids for a moment onboard?*

Even on the family oriented Disney cruise ships, there's always an adults-only area that's free of kids under 16 or so. This usually includes a dedicated pool and hot tub, and in some cases even a bar and dining area. On some upscale cruise lines that cater to an older demographic, many areas feel like they're adult-only that aren't. Bottom line, if you want to be free of your kids or anyone else's, there's always at least one area of the ship to do so.

#48: *Do I need to bring a lot of cash with me?*

It helps but it's not necessary. As stated above, commerce on cruise ships is basically cashless in that you set up an account that's tied to your credit card. You're then given a plastic card that acts as both your room key and debit card while on board. Any transaction onboard uses that card. On some of the new high-tech ships, the cards are being replaced with a wrist band.

If you intended to tip a lot, then it pays to come with a lot of small bills ($1s and $5s). The crew will appreciate it much more as it will go directly to them and not be shared, as are the automatic gratuities charged to your cruise card account.

> *TIP: If you want a lanyard for your cruise card instead of carrying it around, the casino sometimes has them for free at the cashiers window, and kids can get them where they sign up for activities.*

#49: *How do I pay for the things I buy onboard?*

Cruise ships are cashless and everything is charged to your personal account that's tied to your credit card. When you check in you're given a plastic cruise card that acts as both your room key and a debit card for anything that you buy onboard. This covers just about any goods or services, although in some casinos cash still rules to some degree. When you make a purchase, all you do is sign the receipt, just like you would with any other credit card purchase.

Each cruise line calls their card something different. For instance, Carnival calls it the Sign and Sail card, while Royal Caribbean calls it a Sea Pass card.

> *TIP: If you're asked for your card while onboard, whatever you're doing or ordering is probably not free.*

#50: *Do I need to tip while onboard?*

Servers, bartenders, room stewards and waiters all depend upon tips as their main source of income. For that reason most cruise lines automatically include a 15 to 18% tip in any beverage or dining purchase or spa session.

Likewise, passengers can be automatically charged anywhere from $10 to $20 in gratuities per person per day in order to cover your cabin steward, wait staff in the main dining room, and other housekeeping staff.

Many guests feel the automatic amount is insufficient and choose to include either an extra cash tip when the service is rendered, or at the end of the cruise. While it's also possible to add an additional gratuity amount to your onboard account, that tip then goes into a pot that's shared amongst the staff. Cash tips to the individual are much more appreciated.

#51: *Do I have to tip when I buy a drink?*

No, a 15 to 18% tip is automatically added to the price of a drink. You're able to add an additional tip if you're so inclined, just like when you pay for a meal in a restaurant. Many cruisers with drink packages or who receive free drinks thanks to their loyalty tier will add a cash tip for the server to make sure that they're compensated for their work.

#52: *Does the casino take cash or can I use my onboard account?*

Most ship casinos take either cash or your onboard account via your ship card. Some casinos allow you to establish a pre-approved line of credit beforehand. A few ships are cash only, and Disney ships don't even have a casino.

Another way to pay is with casino vouchers or credits that you can purchase beforehand in $25, $50 or $100 increments. You can either use these at the casino or turn them in for cash, although there may be a service charge of up to 5% for doing so. The amount is charged to your credit card as a purchase and not a cash advance, so you can save some on the interest and/or service charge.

Many cruise lines have separate loyalty programs just for the casino, which features rebates depending upon the amount gambled, or free or reduced entry into one of the gambling tournaments.

Be aware that the age limit to be allowed to gamble is different from cruise line to cruise line and even itinerary to itinerary. Sometimes it's 18 and other times its 21. Casinos are usually open about an hour after sailing but may stay open during some port stops.

> *TIP: Remember that you have to cash out any existing casino credits or winnings the last night of your cruise. Credits that are left over will roll over until your next cruise and can't be redeemed by email later.*

#53: Will I have an Internet connection onboard?

Yes, virtually all ships have a wireless network and an Internet cafe available for passengers. It's not cheap and except for some of the newer ships, it's not fast either.

Most ships will have various Internet packages available that range from a per day rate, per cruise rate, or in 30 and 60 minute blocks. Rates aren't cheap at about $0.55 per minute, although that's coming down as some of the newer technology is implemented.

The new technology also means a faster connection, although it will never be as fast as your cable modem at home. In fact, in most cases the speed is similar to the old 56k dial-up modem days. It's good enough for email but will take forever to upload or download a photo. In fact, most photo, music and video sites are blocked, as well as services like Skype.

This is one area where being in the loyalty program really helps, as members are given a discount on Internet connectivity that increases with each higher tier. The highest tier members may even be given free blocks of anywhere from 30 to 90 minutes.

> *TIP: Be careful to note if the block of time is over the length of the cruise and not from the time you sign on. Also remember to sign off when you're finished or you'll continue to rack up the extra minutes in charges.*

#54: *Can someone from back home call me on the ship?*

Yes, but it will cost you. First of all, most ships have a dedicated number that someone from anywhere can call. Of course, the big problem with that is finding you on the ship if you're not in your room, although they can leave a message on your cabin phone. You can also call them back on the line but it will cost around $8 per minute to talk.

A second way is much easier and that's a call to your cell phone. Most cruise lines have a special cellular connection with one of the major carriers that's turned on as soon as the ship gets 12 miles out to sea. Again, it's expensive in that none of the discount roaming programs apply so you're paying anywhere from about $2.50 to $8 per minute.

When the ship is closer than 12 miles to shore, the network is turned off and you're able to connect to the local cell service. Keep in mind that roaming charges are in force and can be just as expensive as those supplied at sea, depending upon your plan and the country you're near.

> *TIP: When you're in port you should be able to connect to the country's local cellular network and be billed at the international roaming rate. Sometimes the ship's network remains on though and overpowers the local network, so make sure that you're aware of the network before you make that call. You may have to leave the ship to get a better rate before you make the call.*

#55: Can I text message while at sea?

Yes, but just like with voice phone calls, the rates can be really steep. An outgoing text can cost you $1.50, and any part of 100mB of data could cost you $25. Incoming text rates are usually only around $0.05, but that's still much more than you're probably paying on your current plan.

The best thing is to always assume that you're paying high sea rates when texting or using data, and know that even International roaming rates can earn you a surprise on your next bill.

#56: *What's tendering?*

Tendering means that the port doesn't have a dock or isn't deep enough to support the draft of the ship, so it must anchor offshore and use smaller boats to transport the passengers to shore. Most tenders hold anywhere from 100 to 200 people, and can take from several minutes to a half-hour to make the journey to port.

Sometimes there's quite a wait to get onto the tender since boarding is slow as only one or two at a time can load from the side of the ship. If you have an early excursion booked, or you're a member of an higher loyalty program tier, then you're usually able to board before anyone else.

#57: *Can I smoke while onboard?*

There used to be far more smoking areas on cruise ships than there are now. Most ships now have a no smoking policy except for dedicated areas. That said, there are more of them than you think.

Most ships dedicate one side of the promenade deck for smokers. You can usually tell by the ash trays, which don't exist on the opposite side. There may also by areas on the pool deck for smokers, usually on the same side of the ship as the smoker's promenade deck. Finally, most ships also have a cigar bar or room where you can easily light up.

One thing you can no longer do is smoke on your balcony if you have a balcony cabin. While you might think that no one can see you, remember there are cameras everywhere, even on the outside of the ship, and anything on fire immediately stands out. You'll probably get a warning at first, but repeated violations could get you kicked off the ship at the next port.

#58: *Can I smoke in the casino?*

On most ships you can smoke in the casino, but there are some that don't allow it (like on Celebrity ships). On some ships you can smoke in the entire casino, while others split it half so smokers and non-smokers alike have their own areas.

#59: *Can I do my laundry onboard?*

You can have your clothes either laundered or dry cleaned for a fee that's on par with your local cleaner. All ships do massive amounts of laundry, so doing a few more pieces is a drop in the bucket to them. In some cases, a discount is provided as part of the loyalty program.

Some ships have self-serve laundromats as well, although I think that's the last thing I'd want to do when on vacation.

> *TIP: If you're opposed to sending your laundry out, a reasonable substitute is to use a large 2.5 gallon ziplock bag. Just pop your clothes in, add water and a dollop of shampoo from the shower, seal, and shake. Wrap the wet clothes in a bath towel and squish it as hard as you can to get the extra water out so it will dry faster, then position it near the air vent using an elastic travel wash line.*

#60: Can kids stay on the ship while the parents go ashore?

Yes, but in many cases its required that they be involved in a ship supervised activity. The good part is that they usually don't seem to mind because its fun and there's so much to do.

#61: Can I get my hair done onboard?

All cruise ships have a hair stylist and beauty shop on board that can accommodate most beauty needs. This is supplied by a third party vendor (usually a company called Steiner, who also hires the message therapists, fitness instructors, nail technicians and receptionists).

#62: Can I get a tour of the ship?

Yes, on most cruises that's possible. The tours fall into two different categories; a ship tour and an entertainment tour. The ship tour generally takes you behind the scenes to the galley, engine room, the laundry and sometimes even the bridge, while the entertainment tour looks at what goes on backstage to put on the various shows. The ship tour is usually given once a cruise and is at the discretion of the captain. While you have to pay for either tour, these are usually free perks that come with the higher loyalty tiers.

#63: *What happens if I buy a bottle of liquor at a port?*

It will be seized by security as you reboard the ship, stored, then given back to you on the last night of the cruise. Remember that when re-embarking the ship at a port stop you have to go through a security scan just like at the airport that will instantly see any bottle you bring back.

#64: *How often are the pools and hot tubs cleaned?*

Both the pools and hot tubs are cleaned every night. Since so many people swim around in a perfect environment for norovirus, the concentration of chemicals used is higher than what you'd use at home.

#65: *When is the pool the least crowded?*

Early morning or late at night, of course, but an ideal time is during the first dining time at 6PM to around 7:30. Most passengers are at dinner and the pools and hot tubs have far fewer people as a result.

#66: *What is the Promenade deck?*

Most ships have a promenade deck, which is a middle deck that has a continuous outside walkway around the ship. It can be used for relaxing, jogging, and walking, as well as a great place to just watch the sea and port life. On most ships one side of the promenade deck is available for smoking. Lifeboats are accessible from this deck.

#67: *What is the Lido deck?*

The lido deck is another name for the pool deck.

#68: *What's the TV like onboard?*

Most cabins have small moveable flat screen televisions that show a variety of television channels, although they are spread out among different cultures. For instance, while there may be a dozen English channels, there also may be four or five Spanish, a few Japanese, and a few Chinese channels as well. The English channels usually consist of several movie channels, a cartoon channel for kids, CNN International, and ESPN International, and perhaps a major US network. And yes, you can catch all the NFL games from a variety of locations onboard, including your room.

The ship will also have a number of dedicated channels consisting of one that just shows a camera from outside the ship, one that shows the a map of the course the ship is on, an information channel about the ship and its activities, and one dedicated to shopping and excursions available at the next port.

Most of the new ships also have huge video monitor like you'd see at a sports stadium on the pool deck. On it you'll see everything from music videos to movies to sporting events. Every night there's usually a new release movie showing, sometimes even with popcorn.

#69: *Will I be able to work out while onboard?*

Yes, almost all ships have a well equipped gym with the latest workout machines and free weights. Most ships also have personal trainers and daily aerobics, yoga and Zumba workouts available too, some free and some for a fee.

#70: *Is a spa session worth it?*

Spa sessions are varied in that they offer everything from Swedish massage to acupuncture treatments to detox wraps to body scrubs. The cost is usually equivalent to a high-end land-based spa, so it's worth it if you're used to paying those prices. Others used to more inexpensive services will find the prices higher than they're used to. Prices for messages are usually far lower in the ports that you'll visit.

> *TIP: If you really want a spa treatment but don't want to pay retail, the spa rates can drop by as much as 30% on embarkation and port days.*

Remember that a 15 to 18% gratuity is automatically added on to the bill, so don't feel that you have to add an additional tip unless you feel that the service was worth the extra.

> *TIP: Most spa workers (who are employed by a third party and not the cruise line, by the way) are trained to try to upsell you into additional products and services at the end of your treatment. If you don't want to hear the spiel, just place a "Please, no upsell" note on the information document that you'll fill out before the service begins.*

#71: *Can I leave the ship before the end of the cruise?*

Surprisingly people leave in the middle a cruise all the time, so neither the crew nor the port staff get too ruffled by it. You have to inform guest relations as to the exact time that you'll be leaving (that's important, it turns out), settle your onboard account where you will be charged for the gratuities for the entire cruise, then a security guard escorts you to the gangway (yes, you'll have to carry your own luggage). There you'll have to sign some paperwork, as you need written permission from the ship to present to the port Cruise Agent and immigration.

At that point you may have to wait there until someone from the port office picks you up and takes you to your own personal customs and immigration inspection. Be aware that some countries like the U.S., Italy and Norway have cabotage laws that restrict foreign flag vessels from transporting guests between one port to another in the same country. That means that if you get on a Cruise at Los Angeles and get off at San Diego without traveling to Ensenada Mexico first, that would violate the Passengers Services Act (commonly called the Jones Act), and the ship will be fined, and that fine will be passed on to you for as much as $300.

That said, dozens of passengers leave in the middle of their cruise every week for various reasons from just about any ship, so it's a fairly easy procedure.

#72: How can I debark faster when we get back to the home port?

You can qualify for the walk-off disembarkation if you carry your baggage with you. On some ships that means you'll be able to get right in line to get off, while on others you may have to wait until the upper tier loyalty club members debark first.

On some ships there are so many people that are trying to debark early that the line wraps halfway around the ship, but even that's faster than waiting until your group number is called later in the morning if your baggage is being handled by the ship. If all goes well you can be off the ship in ten minutes, and even if it's not moving that fast you'll still be off within the hour.

Chapter 6

The Ins and Outs of Cruise Ship Dining

A big part of cruising is eating, and there's usually so much to choose from that it's difficult to decide exactly what to try. On top of that, there's something available to eat just about 24/7 onboard. Here are the answers to the most common questions about cruise dining.

#73: *Will there be something to eat if I'm a vegetarian?*

I'm a vegetarian as well (pescetarian actually) and I never have a problem finding more than enough to eat onboard. The buffet usually has plenty of vegetarian items to choose from and there's always at least one entree every night in the main dining room that's vegetarian. It's a little more difficult if you're a vegan or on a gluten-free diet, but most ships have plenty of offerings for those as well. You can also ask your server in the main dining room for options that the kitchen will gladly provide.

#74: *What's My Time Dining/Dynamic/Free Style Dining?*

Most cruise lines offer an alternative to the scheduled seating in the main dining room which allows you to show up at any time that it's open. You also have the option of calling ahead for a reservation at a particular time.

The good part about this is that you're not tied to the normal dinning times at 6:00 or 8:30PM. The downside of this kind of dining is that you'll probably be seated in a different section of the dining room every night, so you won't be able to have the same wait staff or table mates, if you happen to find some that you really like. The other problem is that there might be a short 10 or 15 minutes wait until you can be seated, although it's usually much shorter than that.

Royal Caribbean is experimenting with what they call Dynamic Dining that does away with the dining room in favor of more restaurants. That means that you can have dinner whenever you'd like, but you may still need a reservation to get the time you'd like, just like at the busy restaurant back home.

#75: *What do I wear to the main dining room?*

On every night except formal night, most main dining rooms allow you to wear pretty much the same thing you'd most likely wear to a nice restaurant at home, which means just about anything but beach wear. Some dining rooms frown on shorts and sandals, but allow you in anyway, while others are insistent that you dress up just a little more. You're safe if you dress "smart casual." That means for men, shorts are okay but not cutoffs, and t-shirts are okay as long as they have sleeves. For the ladies, skirts or pants with a blouse.

#76: *What should I wear to formal night?*

On many ships formal means just that and they expect the women in their finest evening gown and men in a tux or suit and trousers. This used to be the case for all cruise ships but many have relaxed these standards quite a bit, so you'll see some people dressed pretty casually as well as those dressed formally.

What you won't be able to do is dress too casually though, as T-shirts, shorts and sandals will get you pointed to the buffet instead of the main dining room. Be smartly dressed even without being all decked out and you will be welcomed.

That said, many feel that it's fun to dress up and get their picture taken (there are lots of photographers around), since it doesn't happen that often.

#77: *How many formal nights are there?*

On cruises up to five days, only one. On seven day cruises there may be two, although one is also the norm. Between 7 and 13 nights expect two, while 14 to 20 mights expect three. Generally speaking, you can expect a formal night every week for any cruise lasting longer than seven days.

#78: *Can I order more than one main dish in the dinning room?*

The beauty of the main dining room is that you can order whatever you like. If you feel like having two portions of an entree or appetizer, go right ahead and order it (remember this for lobster night). If you want six appetizers and no entree, that's okay too. If you want three helpings of chocolate cake, then more power to you. There are no rules when it comes to dining.

#79: *Do I have to eat in the main dining room every night?*

Not at all. You can eat at one of the specialty restaurants, and many times the buffet has the same dishes that are being served in the dining room. If fact, many people enjoy eating dinner in the buffet because it can be quieter and less hectic than the main dining room.

#80: *What if I can't eat at the specified dining time? Will I miss dinner?*

Probably not, as most cruise ships will do their best to accommodate you. I had this happen to me when I was leaving a cruise early and my departure time was 8PM. I was able to eat dinner at 6:30 even though my normal dining time was set for 8:30.

#81: *What are specialty restaurants?*

The cruise lines have realized that some guests would prefer a more upscale dining experience with more of a restaurant feel, so most cruise ships have specialty restaurants available. These usually specialize in different cuisines, such as a traditional steak house, Italian, Mexican, seafood, Japanese, and just about anything else you can think of. The catch is that it will cost you a flat fee anywhere from $5 to $50 per person extra for the privilege of dining there.

Almost all cruise ships have at least one specialty restaurant available and the larger ones can have as many as 20. In most cases you'll need a reservation to ensure that you'll eat at the time you want.

#82: *What's the Chef's Table?*

The Chef's Table is a private dining experience where you're offered a selected multi-course tasting menu accompanied by paired wines. The dinner may be attended by the executive chef, the food and beverage director, restaurant manager, Maitre d' or head wine steward.

The Chef's Table may only happen once during the course of a cruise and is usually limited to only 10 to 16 guests. The cost may be anywhere from $75 to $150 per person, although it may be less if you're a higher tier member of the loyalty program, or discounted for an early reservation.

The Chef's Table is treated like a formal night in that cocktail dresses, gowns or dressy pantsuits are encouraged for the ladies, and a jacket or sweater with pants for the men. The entire experience can last for two to three hours.

#83: *Can I take food off the ship at a port?*

No, the only things you're allowed to take off the ship are factory sealed items like granola or chocolate bars. In almost all ports it's against the local agriculture laws to take fresh fruit, baked goods, veggies and meat off the ship and in many cases it's punishable with a fine.

Chapter 7

To Love or Hate The Drink Package

Each cruise line offers multiple drink packages that cover both non-alcoholic and alcohol-based drinks or a combination of both. The problem is that these can be confusing in that it's not always easy to decipher what's included in each one. This chapter will attempt to shed a little light on the subject.

#84: *What is a drink or beverage package?*

A drink package means that you pay a flat fee per day for all the beverages you can drink that aren't already available for free. The idea is that you'll save money over the course of the cruise.

First of all be aware that there are many drink packages available and that's what makes it confusing. Each cruise line calls them by different names but what it essentially boils down to is a non-alcoholic drinks package, a wine-only package, and an alcohol drinks package in a variety of variations (that's where it becomes confusing). Some low-end drink packages provide unlimited soft drinks while others just include bottled water. Some include all non-alcoholic drinks from soft drinks, bottled water, specialty coffees, orange juice and alcohol-free cocktails.

Alcohol packages range from wine-only to a limited selection of beer, wine and mixed drinks to everything the ship has to offer both alcoholic and non. The prices can vary from around $5 per day for soft drinks only to as much as $60 per day that includes everything on the ship, to a point. Many drink packages won't cover cocktails or wine over a certain amount (anywhere from $8 to $12), which means that you have to pay the difference for that glass of high-end Chardonnay.

When you sign up for the soft drink package you're usually given a dedicated souvenir cup that allows you to freely refill from one of the soda stations around the ship. If you don't have the cup, you can't use the machine. The other packages are loaded onto your cruise card/room key and will automatically alert the bartender or waiter so you won't be charged.

#85: *Is the drink package worth it?*

To some people it is, but it depends on how much you use it. If you're a big water or soda drinker, then paying $5 to $10 per day can pay off if you have five drinks. Since most mixed drinks on a ship are around $8, it means that you'll need to drink six cocktails per day to get your money's worth. Not a problem for some people and way too much for others.

Keep in mind that you probably won't be able to take advantage of the package as much on port days since you'll most likely be off the ship for at least half the day. It also might not be worth it if you're at one of the upper tiers of the loyalty program and are able to get a number of free drinks at the events in the evening.

Despite the fact that you might not drink enough to cover the daily cost, many still feel that it's worth it because they don't have to worry about how much they're spending during the course of the cruise. The peace of mind makes the expense a sound investment.

#86: *If I have a drink package, do I still need to tip the bartender?*

You don't have to, since gratuities are included in the drink package price. That said, many cruisers with packages leave a dollar tip in cash for the server every time they get a drink just to be sure that they're compensated, and to ensure good service the next time around.

TIP: The bartenders are reassigned every 2 weeks so that surly bartender at the pool bar probably won't be there the next time you cruise on the same ship.

#87: Can I share my drink package?

No, the package is for you only and can't be shared with a spouse, family member, friend or anyone else. That means you can't order two drinks at a time so you can give one away. On many ships there's also a 15 minute interval between drinks so you can't just go up to another bar to get that second drink. The cruise lines want to keep you honest, but it also keeps the price down for everyone if you don't take undo advantage of the program.

#88: Can I buy a drink package onboard or do I have to buy it pre-cruise?

A drink package can be bought beforehand or onboard. In fact, ships aggressively push the drink packages for most of the cruise and will pro rate the cost over the remaining number of days left if you buy it midway through the itinerary. On some ships, packages can no longer be purchased after the halfway point of the cruise.

TIP: It's best to wait until you're on board to purchase a drink package since there may be a discount that won't be available pre-sailing.

Chapter 8

Be Loyal To The Loyalty Program

Just like the airlines, every cruise line offers a loyalty program to keep repeat customers coming back. These programs work very much the same as they do with a major airline except the perks are different, and some say even better, especially at the highest levels. Here are answers to some of the most common loyalty program questions.

#89: How does a cruise line loyalty program work?

All loyalty programs are broken into tiers with a passenger reaching a certain level based upon the amount of points that have been accrued. Most loyalty programs have more similarities to each other than differences. They're all based on the amount of time spent cruising, the perks increase with the tier, and the benefits center around free or discounted goods or services.

That said, here's generally what you can expect from any program:
- Discounts and upgrades
- Faster embarkation and debarkation
- Free services and amenities
- Gifts and swag

The biggest differences between the programs are at the level that most of the desirable perks actually kick in. Let's take a look at Carnival's Very Important Fun Person Club (VIFP) as an example.

Carnival's five-tier VIFP Club is available to all passengers, even the ones that haven't sailed yet. Your tier ranking is based on the number of days you've sailed with Carnival, and is broken out as follows:

Blue – Never sailed through the first sailing

Red – Up to 24 cruise days

Gold – 25 to 74 days

Platinum – 75 to 199 days

Diamond – 200 days and up

Benefits: Benefits start with a free bottle of water, and progress to include priority check-in, boarding, debarkation, tender boarding, restaurant and spa reservations. The higher levels include VIFP parties, member pins, free laundry, casino discounts, and complimentary specialty restaurant meals. There's even a one-time free cabin upgrade or free fares for third and fourth passengers in one cabin.

As with most programs, the perks get better for those who cruise more. For instance, members who sail on their 25th, 50th and 75th Carnival cruises (not days) receive shipboard credits of 25, 50 or 75 percent of the cruise fare paid, respectively. On the 100th cruise, you become eligible for a complimentary Caribbean, Mexican Riviera or Alaska voyage of up to eight days.

The biggest downside to the program is that significant benefits really don't kick in until you hit Platinum.

Members-Only Deals: Cruise price specials are offered to all past passengers but many times they're really not much of a bargain. As with other program's cruise discounts, you may be able to get a better rate by shopping around.

#90: *Is there a way that I can upgrade to the next tier quickly?*

If you really want to jump levels fast there are ways to do it. One is to book suite level cabins, which provide additional points. On many cruise lines, a suite is good for double points but on others it could go to 10 times that, if you can afford it.

Another is to cruise solo, which generally provides double the points, since you're paying for two. If you're lucky enough to get a single supplement deal of 150% (meaning that the second fare is half-price), you'll usually still receive your double points but for a lot less money.

In many cases just sailing in a suite is enough to get basically the same perks as an elite level loyalty member, although only for that cruise. The one exception on some cruise lines are the junior suites in that some only receive partial suite benefits since many cruise lines consider them more of a premium balcony rather than a small suite. Regardless, booking a junior suite is an excellent way to double your cruise points at a reasonable price.

#91: *Can I use the cruise line branded credit card to get more loyalty club points?*

Many cruise lines have their own Visa or MasterCharge cards that also accrue loyalty club points when you use it, just like with an airline card. That sounds pretty good on the surface, but many times the points aren't exactly transferrable and aren't worth as much as you're led to believe, so it's not a reliable way to accrue points. Many times the credit card points are only good for onboard credit and have no bearing on your loyalty program tier, so it's best to read the fine print before you jump in.

#92: *What is the Welcome Back party?*

Most cruise lines will have a Welcome Back party on board for their loyalty club members where they serve free drinks and appetizers. These are usually attended by the ship's captain and senior staff officers, who are available for any questions.

Welcome Back parties are all pretty typical in that the cruise director acts as the master of ceremonies, and the captain is the main attraction. Many captains have a canned speech while others are very loose and will ad lib and take questions from the audience.

At the beginning of the show the cruisers from all the tiers are recognized, with a special presentation to passengers onboard who have sailed the most. I'm always amazed at the number of people that have 1,000 plus nights at sea under their belts, but even more so at the ones that are at 1,700+ (there's seems to be one on every sailing). Imagine that, spending almost five years on vacation!

#93: *What is a loyalty event?*

Many cruise lines provide a nightly event for its higher tier loyalty club members. This could be either in a dedicated private lounge or in one of the ship's bars that is closed off to lower tier loyalty members and non-loyalty passengers. These events typically include free drinks and appetizers.

Chapter 9

What If Something Happens?

99.9% of the time you're going to have a great cruise that will go smoothly with an itinerary that will be met exactly as planned. That said, occasionally something out of the ordinary does occur that can change things. Sometimes you just wonder what would happen if it does. Rest assured, the cruise line has you covered, and this chapter should put your mind at ease.

#94: *What happens if a ship can't make a port because of the weather?*

Many ports, especially ones that are tendered such as Grand Cayman or Belize, are sometimes skipped because of extreme weather conditions like high winds because the passengers would be at risk. Most of the time when that a port is skipped it becomes an extra sea day, and the Cruise Director's staff will schedule alternative activities to keep everyone happy.

If you paid for an excursion, the charge will be refunded to you, as will any port fees that were assessed to your fare. It's highly unlikely that you will receive any additional compensation by the cruise line for a missed port however.

> *TIP: This is one of the times when being on a larger ship is an advantage, as there's far more to do during the sea days, especially if the weather is too cold or windy to be on the pool deck.*

#95: *What happens if I get seasick?*

One of the fears of first-time cruisers is that they'll get seasick (the proper term is motion sickness) sometime during the cruise. Cruise ships are massive and there's very little motion as they drive through the see, so it's highly unlikely that you'll get sick. In fact, I've personally never encountered anyone seasick on a cruise, even through some pretty big storms. That doesn't mean it doesn't happen though.

If you are one of the unlucky few that do get seasick, there are a number of things you can do to find some fast relief. First the "organic" way to treat it without anything medical.

- **Keep moving.** The urge is to lie down, but that can often make the motion sickness even worse because it doesn't help you adapt to the motion of the ship. Motion sickness is a battle of the senses, where the motion you see doesn't agree with what the balance center of your inner ear is feeling. The best way to combat it is to keep moving around to get your sea legs.

- **Avoid anything that requires your eyes to closely focus.** You want to avoid reading, for instance, since that makes the symptoms worse.

- **Look at the horizon**. Either get to a window or go out on deck and use the horizon to gain your equilibrium. *Do Not* stare at the waves. That will make the feeling worse.

- **Get something light in your stomach right away** after the nauseated feeling passes. Something light like crackers or toast will do the trick.

- **For many, ginger really helps**. Ginger snaps, ginger tea, ginger ale, ginger gum or ginger candy can help a lot.

- **Try an acupressure wrist band.** Some people swear by them and will begin to wear them before they ever step onto the ship. A number of these products are available, including the Relief Band and Sea Band.

If the organic way is not your style, the old standby medication used by the cruise lines is called Bonine, which you can get at a pharmacy before hand, or from the ship's purser or onboard hospital. It will cause drowsiness, but you'll feel better. In fact, the hospital will probably have it available outside in the waiting room, so you won't even have to wait for the doctor. The trick is to take it before you get sick though, so if you're prone to motion sickness, take some about an hour before the ship leaves port.

Dramamine is another go-to medication, but it's a lot stronger and will for sure make you sleepy. Once again, it's best to take it to keep from getting sick, instead of as a cure.

Finally, many people swear by the Scopalamine patch, which you wear behind your ear. It provides a continuous small dosage of this anti-nausea drug, but is only available with a doctor's prescription. This does have some limitations in that it can only be worn for three days at a time and may cause blurred vision and headaches.

All that said, you probably won't get seasick, but if you do you have a lot of options to get by it fast.

TIP: If all else fails, go the the ship's doctor, who can give you a big-time antihistamine injection that will fix you up in about 30 minutes and is far more effective than a pill.

#96: What happens if I really get sick or injured while onboard?

Every cruise ship has a hospital and medical staff (including at least one doctor) that's set up to treat common short-term illnesses and minor emergencies. They're not equipped to deal with anything major however, so a patient with a malady that exceeds the limits of their care must be transferred to a hospital on shore.

If that should occur, most cruise ships will either return to the last port, divert to the closest port, or arrange for a helicopter pickup at sea. The latter is a last resort in that it's dangerous enough that it's avoided in all but extreme cases. Most cruise ships are within hours of a port, and it may take the same amount of time to actually get a helicopter there and back.

Shipboard medical emergencies like heart attacks are dealt with very quickly as there is an emergency team in place. You'll usually hear "Alpha, alpha, alpha, deck 4, main dining room," or similar code words over the PA system that tells the team the location of the incident.

For anything minor that doesn't require hospitalization, the onboard medical staff can handle it nicely.

#97: *What happens if I fall overboard?*

Let's get this one out of the way quickly. People just don't fall overboard accidentally. It's not an easy thing to do, and on the very rare occasion when someone does go overboard, it's either because of foul play (usually with a spouse) or because they were excessively drunk and stupid.

Let's put it like this - if you go for a walk around the block, how many times do you fall off the curb? Even if you did fall off once, was it because you were walking normally on the sidewalk? How easy do you think it would be to fall off if each curb had a railing at the edge? Falling doesn't happen much there, and it doesn't happen on a cruise ship either.

Even if you manage to get yourself into a position where this super rare event does occur, there are dozens of cameras that are constantly monitoring the decks and hundreds of people that are gazing out to sea in all directions at the same time that will most likely see you. Every ship constantly drills for such an event, and the crew is very skilled at man-overboard rescues.

That said, you're more likely to be hit by lightening than accidentally fall from a ship.

#98: *What happens if I get norovirus?*

Cruise ships take great care to avoid the spread of Norovirus (a nasty gastrointestinal flu) by constantly sanitizing the common surfaces of the entire ship. Nonetheless, just like schools, hotels and even hospitals, anyplace where several thousand people are in close contact (like a cruise ship) is prime territory for this unhappy bug.

The truth of the matter though, is that very few passengers are effected even during what the federal Center for Disease Control considers a major outbreak. Usually that means less than 1% of a ship's passengers and crew.

For instance, I recently went on a cruise that sailed directly after an outbreak on the previous cruise. On the "norovirus cruise" there were 15 passengers that came down with the bug out of a little over 3,000 on board (not even counting the crew). When the ship returned to its home port, it immediately went into a ship-wide deep sanitation that prevented the next round of passengers from boarding for six hours (much to their chagrin).

On the subsequent cruise, the captain kept everyone informed of the sanitation progress, the crew served everyone at the buffets so no passenger handled food utensils, and good sanitation practices (like washing your hands - still the best preventative) were constantly kept at the forefront. Guess what? No incidents on the next voyage or thereafter.

Even when there hasn't been an outbreak, cruise ships always err on the side of caution when it come to Norovirus. Many cruise lines insist that every passenger use hand sanitizer before entering an eating establishment and have a crew member there to personally spread some sanitizer on your hands when you enter. I've seen passengers forbidden to go into a dining area unless they used some sanitizer on their hands.

That said, if you're unlucky enough to get the virus at the beginning of a cruise, you'll find yourself quarantined inside your cabin for 4 to 6 days until you're no longer contagious. Unfortunately there are no medications that can be taken for the virus, except for plenty of fluids to stave off dehydration. You just have to suffer through it and let it run its course.

#99: *What happens if we sail through a hurricane?*

Many of the least expensive cruises in the Caribbean are offered during the hurricane season, which officially begins on June 1st, but is the worst between the beginning of September and the end of November.

Usually when a hurricane does pop up in the path of your cruise, the ship will make every effort to sail around it and stay as far away as possible. Keep in mind that the captain would never do anything to put the ship, his passengers, or crew in danger, so he will alter its course to keep everyone safe.

If the hurricane happens to be in the path of one of your ports of call, the itinerary will be changed to another port or a day at sea. It may not be the vacation you expect, but it might even be better too.

Unless you're in the middle of a hurricane, the weather will be no different than at any other time. Hurricane season simply means that conditions are favorable for the formation of those storms, otherwise it's business as usual for Mother Nature and the cruise line!

#100: *Will the ship sink if it's hit by a rogue wave?*

A rogue wave is classified as a wave that's two times the average of the biggest wave in a given area of sea. For years the idea of a rogue wave was thought to be a myth, but they do indeed occur on rare occasions, and a cruise ship is as vulnerable as any other oceangoing vessel. That said, even the biggest one ever recorded won't capsize a modern cruise ship.

For instance, in 2014 a 40 foot wave hit Royal Caribbean's Grandeur of the Seas, which knocked out some windows in the dinning room, soaked the rug. and damaged a lifeboat. The dining room was back up and running for the next meal, and most passengers weren't even aware that it occurred.

Rogue waves do happen, and they happen more frequently that you might think, but that's still very rare. Once again, the chances are slim that it will affect your vacation greatly.

#101: *What happens if the ship is attacked by pirates?*

This one is very unlikely to happen since most pirates are nowhere near where cruise ships go, and the captain will take a wide berth of any known recent activity if possible.

That said, if there ever is an attack, the crew is very well drilled on how to repel it. This includes evasive maneuvers by the captain (a cruise ship at flank speed that's zig zagging through the water is darn near impossible to board) to water canons. Don't forget the crew is over 1,000 strong, not to mention the able bodied passengers. Not an easy task for any pirate.

#102: *What happens if I miss the ship during a port stop?*

Now here's something that does happen more than occasionally. You're in port having a nice chilled cocktail and you think you still have an hour before the ship sets sail, only to hear the wailing of its air horn as it leaves the port and you behind. You look at your watch and it says 4PM but you know that the ship leaves at 5. What happened?

This is something that confuses cruisers a lot, even the veterans. The ship's time doesn't automatically correspond to shore time, therefore, you must always be sure to stay on the same time as the ship. There isn't a time discrepancy all the time, but it does happen, and you'll usually be warned via an announcement before you leave the ship (the security team may remind you as you debark as well) or a notice in the daily newsletter or schedule of activities.

The captain can set sail at any time after the designated departure time, but will usually wait as long as possible before it impacts his schedule. If you're on an excursion (especially one purchased on the ship), the excursion manager will always call ahead if there's a delay and the ship will wait, but if they don't hear from you, you're on your own and are responsible for getting either to the next port to meet the ship or going back home.

That sounds horrible enough, but there still could be complications involved. You probably left your passport locked in the safe in your room, so all you have is your photo ID and ship's ID card. At this point the Ship's Agent at the port will take over. Sometimes the ship will offload both your passport and luggage so you're not totally stranded, but that's not always a given.

That said, the Ship's Agent will help you contact the local US Consulate to get another passport so you can travel. It helps a lot if you have a copy of it on a file on your phone (password protect it!), or even the passport number, but it's not totally necessary. Your ship's ID card will verify that you were on the ship so you won't get hassled by Immigration.

That's one of the reasons why you should always have the Ship's Agent's phone number when you go ashore. It will be printed on the daily cruise newsletter that the ship provides (although it's usually in small print so you have to look hard). If you know you're going to be late for any reason, call the Agent, who will then contact the ship. At that point they will make every effort to wait for you, but there's no guarantee it will wait as long as you need to get back. That said, they will at least let the Agent know that you'll require assistance, and hopefully even get your passport to them, so at least that part of your next hassle will be avoided.

TIP: When in doubt of the time, check one of the ship's many clocks and synchronize your watch or phone before you leave the ship.

Chapter 10

What About The Crew?

The crew is a big part of the cruising experience, but there's usually so little that we know about the people that facilitate our vacation on the sea. Here are a few questions that you might have about the people that we see and the ones that we don't that get us to a different port every day with the greatest of ease.

#103: *What's the hierarchy on the ship?*

There is definitely a division in work responsibilities onboard a cruise ship, and those responsibilities also define the privileges as well. There are three distinct worker classes on a cruise ship: officers, staff, and crew. While staff and crew generally refer to the ship's workers, the difference is that staff tend to have managerial or skilled duties while the crew tend to be worker bees who do, for want of a better word, the "chores" of the ship like maintenance, housekeeping, kitchen and waitstaff.

The crew eat, sleep and live on the two crew-only decks when they're off-duty, and are only allowed to enter the passenger areas when working. They are forbidden from interacting with the passengers unless on the job, although they may do so if on shore together and contact is initiated by a passenger.

The staff have it better in that they're allowed the run of the ship, and may even be allowed to have a cocktail in a ship bar, dine in one of the restaurants, take in a show, or even sunbathe at one of the guest pools during a port day when most passengers are on shore. That said, any of these perks are only available after the passengers have been accommodated.

One of the downsides to this is that staff members must wear their uniforms at all times when not on a crew deck, so any time they step into the passenger area they become the face of the ship and are on the job, and therefore must smile and be cheerful. Most staffers want some relief from having to be "on" all the time so they tend to stay in the crew area when off duty.

The exception to the staff having to wear uniforms all the time is the entertainers. Although many sometimes have additional ship duties beyond simply entertaining (muster drill management, for instance), they are considered "non-striped" officers and are allowed to mingle with the guests more freely.

The other perk they enjoy is that they are able to hang out with the officers as well. Other than that, fraternization between officers and crew is forbidden with one exception - the crew bar. There the highest ranking officers can party with the lowest men and women on the totem pole, although this occurs infrequently since there's usually a separate "officers only" bar on most ships as well.

#104: *How much does the crew get paid?*

Cruisers always wonder about how much members of the crew gets paid. After some research, I've come up with the approximate monthly salaries for the officers and even some of the staff. Keep in mind that the figures cited vary from cruise line to cruise line, and greatly depend upon how large the vessel is.

Deck Crew

Captain - $10,000 per month and up

Staff Captain (the executive officer) - $7,000 per month and up

First Officer - $5,000 to $8,000 per month

Second Officer - $4,000 to $7,000 per month

Third Officer - $3,000 to $5,000 per month

Chief Security Officer - $4,000 to $7,000 per month

Security Crew - $1,000 to $1,500 per month

Engineering

Chief Engineer - $8,000 per month and up

Assistant Chief Engineer - $7,000 per month and up

Environmental Officer - $6,000 to $9,000

First Engineering Officer - $7,000 to $9,000 per month

Engineering Cadet - $1,500 to $2,500 per month

First Plumber - $1,200 to $3,300 per month

Technical Clerk - $1,000 to $1,800 per month

Engine Crew- $600 to $800 per month

Hotel

Hotel Manager - $7,000 and up per month

Cruise Director - $5,800 to $7,500 and up per month

Assistant Cruise Director - $2,500 to $3,000 per month

Cruise Director Staff - $1,800 to $2,300 per month

Casino Manager - $2,400 to $4,200 per month

Disk Jockey - $1,700 to $2,000 per month

Comedian - $1,600 to $2,400 per month

Singer, Dancer, Musician - $1,600 to $3,000 per month

Guest Entertainer - $3,800 to $7,000 and up per month

Fitness Instructor - $1,900 to $2,000 per month

Shore Excursions Manager - $2,300 to $3,600 per month

Accountant - $3,400 to $3,600 per month

Executive Chef - $4,500 to $8,000 per month

First Cook - $1,900 to $2,500 per month

Head Waiter - $2,800 to $3,200 per month

Waiter - $1,200 to $2,000 per month (mostly via tips)

Assistant Waiter - $1,000 to $1,500 per month (mostly via tips)

Bartender - $1,000 to $1,500 per month (mostly via tips)

Message Therapist - $2,800 to $3,600 per month (mostly via tips)

Executive Housekeeper - $4,000 to $7,000 per month

Food and Beverages Manager - $5,000 to $8,000 per month

Photographer - $1,800 to $2,800 per month

Laundry Man/Linen Keeper - $700 to $900 per month

Utility Cleaner - $600 to $800 per month

Dishwasher - $500 to $700 per month

Galley Cleaner - $500 to $700 per month

Medical

Chief Medical Officer - $8,000 and up

Nurse - $4,000 to $6,000 per month

#105: *Some of the crew is paid so little. Are they being taken advantage of?*

You expect the captain, executive chef or hotel manager to be well paid and they are, but when you look at many of the above salaries, it seems like some of the crew are being severely taken advantage of. For a laborer, busboy or dishwasher to make $600 per month seems like a crime, but in the country they came from this can actually be quite a good salary and a step up the economic ladder. In fact, $600 a month may be more than the average person in their country makes in a year.

Many crew members support their entire families back home as they send all of their monthly paycheck back, since they have virtually no expenses while on board. Many even manage to save enough to buy very nice houses in their homeland and are even able to retire when they tire of the daily cruise routine and end that final contract.

That said, many crew members that face the public (like waiters, bartenders and cabin attendants) are very dependent on gratuities as they have a very low base pay. Although most cruise lines charge passengers a minimum per day gratuity that covers their housekeepers and waiters ($12 is the current norm), leaving that extra $10 or $20 that you probably won't miss is a huge deal for those that depend on it.

You'll not find anyone complain about these tip-dependent jobs though, and for the most part they're quite sought after since they can be a step up the financial ladder for some. The cruise lines can get away with paying these low salaries because their ships are bound by the laws of the country that the ship is registered in, which is known as the Flag of Convenience or FOC (take notice most ships are registered in Liberia, Panama or the Bahamas). The ownership and offices may be in another country, but the FOC labor laws will be far less stringent. In the cruise line's view, this keeps the part of the crew that's reliant on tips always smiling in front of its guests.

Even staff in higher paying positions can make out well during the course of a cruise contract. Since everything is provided for, from food to laundry to entertainment to medical and prescriptions, a crew member can make out much better than their land-based friends if they choose to be frugal for duration of their contract.

#106: *Where does the crew stay?*

Crew accommodations are free, but the cabins are mostly spartan at best, even for some of the officers. The lowest level or entry-level workers (including the cooks, waiters, busboys, bartenders, housekeepers and maintenance), who are usually from the third world and may not speak much

English, are placed four to a room on the level just below the waterline on what's known as "B Deck."

These rooms are furnished similarly to guest cabins, but they're smaller with more beds in them. They also have a small television which has the same channels as the passenger cabins, plus one or two dedicated crew channels featuring a variety of sporting events from crew home countries. On modern cruise ships, all crew cabins also have a bathroom, unlike the shared community facilities so hated on older ships.

Most of the staffers (entertainers, casino and spa workers, "shoppies" that work the gift shops, art auctions and photography, and even lower ranked officers) live on the "A Deck," which is at the waterline. These crew members live two or one (if you're a senior staff member) to a cabin, with small single beds and private bathrooms. Generally speaking, the higher the rank, the better the accommodations. The crew also has their own cabin stewards to help keep the rooms respectable, as there are regular inspections from both their managers and officers not only to maintain order but to look for things that need repair.

A typical cruise ship may have multiple crew mess halls, normally one for staff and one or maybe two for the crew.

There may be multiple crew mess halls because of cuisine preferences of different nationalities, where one focuses primarily on Asian-style cuisine and the other more American/European, and there is usually yet another mess hall for the officers. There are also public rooms, a gym, Internet cafe, the famous crew bar, and even a crew swimming pool. There's little time for boredom, as there's also plenty of crew activities after work, with frequent movie nights, theme parties, and even language and business education courses and certifications provided.

There's also a surprisingly well-stocked crew-only store that has everything from toiletries to beer, and it's all at reasonable prices. The crew is also allowed to buy gifts from the passenger stores at a discount (20 to 25% depending upon the cruise line), but only during certain hours when not in conflict with the passengers.

#107: *Can I go to the crew bar?*

Not a chance. The crew is not allowed to fraternize with the passengers, and the passengers are forbidden from entering any crew area. Violating this rule could lead to immediate dismissal of the crew member at the next port with no way home, so you can bet that they won't make that mistake.

#108: *Does the crew get the weekend off?*

Most crew members are expected to work every single day for the length of their contracts. They get time off every day, but not full days. Some crew members, like entertainers, may not work every day but the amount of time they must work is specified in their contracts.

#109: *Can the crew eat leftover passenger food?*

Sometimes. If the food hasn't left the galley (which is most likely desserts), then it may be made available to the crew. They can never eat anything left over from the passengers however, and a crew member can be fired if caught eating passenger food.

Free eBook Bonus!

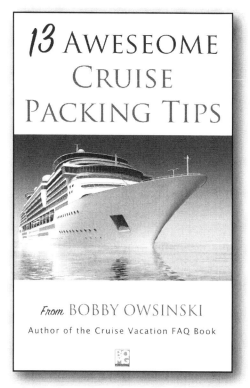

Before you pack for your next cruise, be sure to download this free ebook. It will give you lots of hints about how to pack light, yet still take everything you need.

And what's best is that there's a whole list of things to include that will make you trip a lot easier.

Remember, it's FREE. Just click on this link:

CruiseFrenzy.com

About Bobby Owsinski

Bobby Owsinski has taught thousands of entrepreneurs the principles of branding and social media in his coaching courses, and is one of the best selling authors in the music industry with 23 books that are now staples in business programs in colleges around the world. He's also a contributor to Forbes, his popular blogs have passed 5 million visits, and he's appeared on CNN and ABC News as a music branding expert. Many of his books have also been turned into video courses that can be found online at lynda.com, and he continues to provide presentations, workshops and master classes at conferences and universities worldwide.

Bobby loves to cruise and is nearing the Diamond Plus level on the Royal Caribbean loyalty program. He frequently books cruises around his many lectures if they occur in a port city.

Bobby's blogs are some of the most influential and widely read in the music business. Visit Bobby's production blog at bobbyowsinskiblog.com/, his Music 3.0 music industry blog at music3point0.com, his podcast at bobbyoinnercircle.com and his website at bobbyowsinski.com.

Other Books By Bobby Owsinski

Abbey Road To Ziggy Stardust [with Ken Scott] (ISBN - 978-0739078587 Alfred Music Publishing)

The Mixing Engineer's Handbook 3rd Edition (ISBN #128542087X Course Technology PTR)

The Recording Engineer's Handbook 3rd Edition (ISBN #1285442016 Course Technology PTR)

The Mastering Engineer's Handbook 3rd Edition (ISBN #1598634496 - Course Technology PTR)

Music 4.1: A Survival Guide For Making Music In The Internet Age (ISBN #1423443438 Hal Leonard)

The Drum Recording Handbook 2nd Edition [with Dennis Moody] (ISBN #1423443438 Hal Leonard)

How To Make Your Band Sound Great *with DVD* (ISBN #1423441907 Hal Leonard)

The Studio Musician's Handbook *with DVD* [with Paul ILL] (ISBN #1423463412 Hal Leonard)

The Music Producer's Handbook 2nd Edition (ISBN 978-1423474005 Hal Leonard)

The Musician's Video Handbook *with DVD* (ISBN 978-1423484448 Hal Leonard)

Mixing And Mastering With T-Racks: The Official Guide (ISBN 978-1435457591 Course Technology PTR)

The Touring Musician's Handbook *with DVD* (ISBN 978-1423492368 Hal Leonard)

The Ultimate Guitar Tone Handbook *with DVD* [with Rich Tozzoli] (ISBN 978-0739075357 Alfred Music Publishing)

The Studio Builder's Handbook *with DVD* [with Dennis Moody] (ISBN - 978-0739077030 Alfred Music Publishing)

The Audio Mixing Bootcamp *with DVD* (ISBN - 978-0739082393 Alfred Music Publishing)

Audio Recording Basic Training *with DVD* (ISBN - 978-0739086001 Alfred Music Publishing)

Social Media Promotion For Musicians *The Manual For Marketing Yourself, Your Band or your Music Online* (ISBN - 978-0-9888391-1-3 BOMG Publishing)

Social Media Promotion For Small Business and Entrepreneurs *The Manual for Marketing Yourself or your Business Online* (ISBN - 978-0-9888391-3-7 BOMG Publishing)

Deconstructed Hits: Classic Rock Vol. 1 (ISBN - 978-0739093894 Alfred Music Publishing)

Deconstructed Hits: Modern Pop & Hip-Hop (ISBN - 978-0739073438 Alfred Music Publishing)

Deconstructed Hits: Modern Rock & Country (ISBN - 978-0739073421 Alfred Music Publishing)

The PreSonus StudioLive Mixer Official Manual (ISBN - 978-1470611286 Alfred Music Publishing)

You can get more info and read excerpts from each book by visiting the excerpts section of bobbyowsinski.com.

Bobby Owsinski Lynda.com Video Courses

Social Media Basics for Musicians and Bands

Bookmarking Sites for Musicians and Bands

Pinterest for Musicians and Bands

Google+ for Musicians and Bands

Blogging Strategies for Musicians and Bands

YouTube for Musicians and Bands

Twitter for Musicians and Bands

Mailing List Management for Musicians and Bands

Website Management for Musicians and Bands

Facebook for Musicians and Bands

The Audio Mixing Bootcamp

Audio Recording Techniques

Mastering For iTunes

Audio Mastering Techniques

Music Studio Setup and Acoustics

Selling Music Merchandise

Selling Your Music: CDs, Streams and Downloads

Bobby Owsinski Coaching Courses

BobbyOwsinskiCourses.com
101MixingTricks.com

Bobby Owsinski's Social Media Connections

Music Production Blog: bobbyowsinskiblog.com

Music Industry Blog: music3point0.com

Inner Circle Podcast: bobbyoinnercircle.com

Facebook: facebook.com/bobby.owsinski

Forbes blog: forbes.com/sites/bobbyowsinski/

YouTube: youtube.com/user/polymedia

Linkedin: linkedin.com/in/bobbyo

Twitter: @bobbyowsinski

Website: bobbyowsinski.com